BE LIKE BILL

The Internet's Smartest Sensation

Eugeniu Croitoru & Debabrata Nath

Andrews McMeel
PUBLISHING®

Be Like Bill

Andrews McMeel Publishing
a division of Andrews McMeel Universal
1130 Walnut Street, Kansas City, Missouri 64106

www.andrewsmcmeel.com

17 18 19 20 21 SDB 10 9 8 7 6 5 4 3 2 1

ISBN: 978-1-4494-8347-0

Library of Congress Control Number: 2016958080

First published in Great Britain by Ebury Press, an imprint of Ebury Publishing, a Penguin Random House Group Company

ATTENTION: SCHOOLS AND BUSINESSES
Andrews McMeel books are available at quantity discounts with bulk purchase for educational, business, or sales promotional use. For information, please e-mail the Andrews McMeel Publishing Special Sales Department: specialsales@amuniversal.com.

This is Bill.

Bill started as just another meme on the Internet. But he was unique in that he tried to make people laugh by addressing everyday issues many notice but are too scared to mention.

Bill went viral, since millions could relate to what he felt and said on his Facebook page, OfficialBLB. He even made the news!

Bill isn't afraid to poke fun at himself and others. He knows life is short but there's always time for good manners and laughter.

Bill hopes this book will bring you both.

Be smart.
Be like Bill.

This is Bill.

Bill reads books.

Bill is smart.
Be like Bill.

This is Bill.

Bill wakes up and sees it's snowing outside.

Bill doesn't feel the urge to post a status about it on Facebook because he knows his friends also have windows.

Bill is not a douche.

Be like Bill.

This is Bill.

Bill owns a car.

He knows his car came with a thing called turn signals.

Bill uses those when he is changing lanes.

Bill is a good driver.

Be like Bill.

This is Bill.

Bill is having a conversation on his phone.

Bill doesn't shout because he knows his friend will hear him without using the phone in that way.

Bill is self-aware.
Be like Bill.

This is Bill.

Bill is on Facebook.

He sees a post claiming to give away a free iPhone 6 to anyone who clicks on a link.

Bill knows the only thing he'll get by doing that is a virus.

He reports the post and moves on.

Bill is tech-savvy.
Be like Bill.

This is Bill.

Bill likes watching a particular TV show.

His friends don't like the same show.

Bill doesn't try to force it upon them as he respects their choices.

Bill isn't annoying.

Be like Bill.

This is Bill.

Bill has a child.

Bill understands his child gets one year older on his birthday every year.

Bill can believe it.
Be like Bill.

This is Bill.

Bill bought a sheep.

He named it Relation.

Bill now has a "relationsheep."

Bill is funny.
Be like Bill.

This is Bill.

Bill realizes tomorrow is Monday.

He doesn't post a rant about this on social media.

Bill knows Monday comes every single week.

Bill deals with it. Be like Bill.

This is Bill.
Bill only has one face.
This one.
Bill isn't two-faced.
Be like Bill.

This is Bill.

Bill likes to listen to music.

Bill uses headphones because he knows not everyone might enjoy it, especially on the 6 a.m. train he's traveling on.

Bill is considerate. Be like Bill.

This is Bill.

Bill is on Facebook like the rest of us.

He just uploaded a new profile picture.

Bill didn't like his own profile picture.

Bill is smart.
 Be like Bill.

This is Bill.

Bill only has one Bella.

Bill is a real man.
Be like Bill.

This is Bill.

Bill uses social networking websites.

Bill knows there are some things he should keep private and not share on social media sites for the whole world to see.

Bill cares about his privacy.

Be like Bill.

This is Bella.

Bella actually suggests a restaurant instead of saying "anywhere is fine" when Bill asks her where she wants to eat.

Bella is smart.
Be like Bella.

This is Bill.

Bill has a friend who wears glasses.

He doesn't ask him how many fingers he has up when his friend takes them off.

Bill isn't a douche.
Be like Bill.

This is Bill.

Bill just saw a popular movie that everyone is excited about.

Bill doesn't post spoilers from the movie on social media sites and ruin the experience for others.

Bill knows he is better than that.

Be like Bill.

This is Bill.

Bill doesn't care about someone's religion, nationality, skin color, or ideas.

Bill just hates everyone.

Be like Bill.

This is Bill.

Bill's girlfriend just broke up with him.

He doesn't stalk her on social media sites.

He knows it is only going to hurt him more.

Bill tries to move on.
Be like Bill.

This is Bill.

Bill loves watching other people playing video games.

People make fun of Bill, but Bill doesn't care because he does something
he likes.

Bill knows his
own mind.
Be like Bill.

This is Bill.

Bill doesn't get mad at his friends when they play a prank on him.

He knows they are his friends and that's what friends do.

Bill doesn't take life so seriously.

Be like Bill.

This is Bill.

Bill is waiting for the train.

When it's time to get on, Bill waits for other people to get off first.

Bill knows the basic rules.

Be like Bill.

This is Bill.

Bill is on Facebook.

Bill doesn't post song lyrics with zero context because nobody wants to decode his life through Kanye lyrics.

Bill lives in the real world.

Be like Bill.

This is Bill.

Bill is watching football.

Bill doesn't shout at the TV during the game.

He is aware that the players on the field cannot hear him.

Bill isn't obnoxious.

Be like Bill.

This is Bill.

Bill sees an old video on YouTube that people still watch.

But he doesn't write the comment, "Like if you're watching in 2017."

Bill knows that makes no bloody sense.

Bill is smart.
Be like Bill.

This is Bill.

Bill knows his personal life and happiness are more important than work.

Bill works to live and does not live to work.

Bill maintains a balance.

Be like Bill.

This is Bill.

Bill meets a girl on Facebook.

He doesn't ask for nudes.

Bill is respectful.
Be like Bill.

This is Bill.

Bill wants to serve his country.

Bill applies for the military but he fails.

Bill isn't heartbroken and applies for the police force instead.

Bill does not give up on his dreams.

Be like Bill.

This is Bill.

Bill took sick leave from work today.

Bill doesn't upload selfies and write statuses on Facebook all day.

He knows his coworkers will see them.

Bill isn't stupid.

Be like Bill.

This is Bill.

Bill is on Instagram.

Bill sees a picture of his friend making a duck face.

Bill gives her pieces of bread the next day.

Bill is smart.
Be like Bill.

This is Bill.

Bill is very quiet when he goes to work in the morning because he knows it's really early and other people are still sleeping.

Bill is thoughtful.
Be like Bill.

This is Bill.

Someone speeds past him on the road while he is driving.

Bill doesn't follow them in the hope of insulting their driving.

Bill knows that is dangerous.

Be like Bill.

This is Bill.

Bill has a young child.

Bill doesn't post a message on Facebook telling his son how much he loves him because he knows he doesn't have an account and can't read.

Bill shares his feelings with his kid privately instead.

Be like Bill.

This is Bill.

Bill sometimes gets hate and insults.

Bill just doesn't care, he keeps sipping his tea.

Bill is smart.

Be like Bill.

This is Bill.

Bill goes to work.

Bill doesn't steal pens at work just because he can.

Bill isn't immature like that.

Be like Bill.

This is Bill.

Bill doesn't have anything to say this time.

Sometimes you just have to shut the hell up.

Bill knows that.
Be like Bill.

This is Bill.

Bill has a smartphone with a front-facing camera.

Bill doesn't spend the entire day clicking selfies with it and posting them on social media sites.

He knows that annoys the living hell out of his friends.

Bill has a functioning brain.

Be like Bill.

This is Bill.

Bill is rich.

Despite this, Bill doesn't show off his money.

Bill respects other people who aren't as lucky as him.

Be like Bill.

This is Bella.

Bella doesn't go to the corner shop in her pajamas.

Bella has self-respect.
Be like Bella.

This is Bill.

Bill is on Facebook.

Bill knows if he does not like a picture or say "amen" that people won't die, orphaned children in Africa won't get cancer, and he won't get bad luck for the next million years.

Bill isn't gullible.
Be like Bill.

This is Bill.

Bill is not a warrior.

So he doesn't act like one behind a keyboard.

Bill is smart.

Be like Bill.

This is Bill.

When Bill wants to ask for something he says "please."

When Bill receives something he says "thank you."

Bill has manners.
Be like Bill.

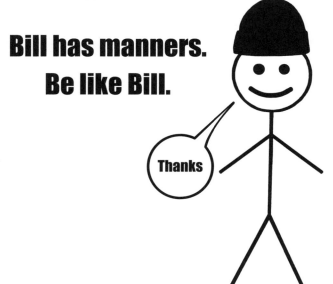

This is Bill.

Sometimes people say or do horrible things to Bill.

Bill's far too wise to react.

Bill lets his old friend *karma* deal with it.

Bill is smart.
Be like Bill.

This is Bill.

When Bill speaks to somebody, he looks into their eyes.

Bill isn't afraid.
Be like Bill.

This is Bill.

Bill makes new friends but at the same time he doesn't neglect his old ones.

Bill cares.

Be like Bill.

This is Bill.

Bill is having dinner.

Bill chews with his mouth closed because he doesn't want to look like a llama.

Bill is polite.
Be like Bill.

This is Bill.

Bill can be nice to people.

That doesn't mean Bill is flirting with them.

Bill is just friendly.

Be like Bill.

This is Bill.

Bill takes a shower every day.

This is because Bill doesn't want to stink like a wet dog.

Bill smells nice.
Be like Bill.

This is Bill.

Bill doesn't cycle on the road when there is a bike path.

Bill uses the path.

Bill isn't ignorant.
Be like Bill.

This is Bill.

Bill has a cold.

Bill doesn't feel the need to tell Facebook, Twitter, and Instagram about it.

Bill is smart.
Be like Bill.

This is Bill.

Bill is filming his baby climbing on the sofa.

He notices the baby is about to fall.

Bill doesn't carry on filming.

He goes and helps the baby.

Bill is responsible.

Be like Bill.

This is Bill.

Bill has a girlfriend.

Despite this, Bill doesn't post pics of them making out, because he knows it annoys some friends.

Bill is respectful.

Be like Bill.

This is Bella.

Bella has a boyfriend who buys her a lot of expensive gifts.

Bella doesn't take photos of every single item with the caption "Lucky Girl."

She knows that would make her a show-off.

Bella isn't a show-off.
Be like Bella.

This is Bill.

Bill just bought a new car.

Bill doesn't take selfies in it, with it, or under it.

Bill is smart.

Be like Bill.

This is Bill.

Bill doesn't have a nose.

This is to avoid sticking it into other people's business.

Be like Bill.

This is Bill.

Bill does not Snapchat his daily life all day, every day.

Bill is not an attention seeker.

Be like Bill.

This is Bill.

Bill doesn't complain to cashiers about the price of things in stores because he knows there's nothing they can do about it.

Bill is not a whining moron.

Be like Bill.

This is Bill.

If Bill promises something, Bill keeps his promise.

Bill is loyal.
Be like Bill.

This is Bill.

Bill has a girlfriend.

Bill also has a smartphone.

He gives more time to his girlfriend than his smartphone.

Bill is caring.

Be like Bill.

This is Bill.

Bill has a quiet friend.

He doesn't always ask his friend why he's being quiet.

Bill knows some people are born to be quiet.

Bill is considerate.

Be like Bill.

This is Bill.

Bill doesn't pee all over a public toilet because he knows other people might need to use the toilet too.

Bill isn't a douche.

Be like Bill.

This is Bill.

Bill isn't afraid to try out new things because he might fail.

He knows without failing one can never truly succeed.

Bill takes failures in stride.

Bill never gives up.

Be like Bill.

This is Bill.

Bill is feeling sad today but he does not post a status on Facebook about it and tag "Angel Stacy" and 69 others.

Bill knows that's the dumbest possible thing one can do on Facebook.

Bill isn't an idiot.
Be like Bill.

This is Bill.

Bill is driving.

Bill doesn't throw garbage from the car's window.

He likes nature and doesn't litter his city.

Bill is responsible.

Be like Bill.

This is Bill.

Bill has gone to a party.

Uh oh. Looks like Bill has had one shot too many.

Bill calls a cab to drop him home.

Bill doesn't drink and drive, putting himself and others at risk.

Bill is responsible.

Be like Bill.

This is Bella.

Bella has a nice body.

But she doesn't post pictures of herself in her underwear on Facebook.

Bella isn't an exhibitionist.

Be like Bella.

This is Bill.

When Bill meets a friend early in the morning, he just offers him a coffee and doesn't speak too much.

Bill is a good friend.

Be like Bill.

This is Bill.

Bill likes a girl and makes his feelings known to her.

The girl makes it clear that she only likes him as a friend.

Bill moves the hell on and does not fall into the friend-zone trap.

Bill knows when to let go.

Be like Bill.

This is Bill's mom Jill.

Jill knows online games cannot be paused.

She doesn't call Bill while he is playing online and ruin his game.

Jill is a smart mom.

Be like Jill.

This is Bill.

Bill owns a dog.

He takes his canine friend for walks rather than just posting its picture on social media sites.

Bill actually cares.

Be like Bill.

This is Bill.

If Bill doesn't know anything about something, he doesn't speak about it.

Bill is smart.
Be like Bill.

This is Bill.

Bill has a lovely girlfriend.

He doesn't touch her bottom in public.

Bill only does that at home.

Bill is a gentleman.

Be like Bill.

This is Bill.

Bill uses instant messaging apps.

He just got a message saying that he will die tomorrow if he does not forward the message to 100 people.

Bill laughs knowing that he would have died at least 1,000 times by now if this were true.

Bill is smart.
Be like Bill.

This is Bill.

Sometimes he likes to go to his backyard, cover himself in dirt, and pretend he is a carrot.

Bill is weird.

Be like Bill.

This is Bill.

Bill sees an old lady enter the bus.

He stands up from his seat and offers it to her.

Bill is considerate.

Be like Bill.

This is Bill.

It's his birthday today but he doesn't post an "It's my birthday today" status on Facebook.

Bill knows Facebook already notifies his friends about it.

Bill isn't an attention seeker.

Be like Bill.

This is Bella.

Bella is on Facebook.

She doesn't check into a hospital every time she is at one.

Bella is not a drama queen.

Be like Bella.

This is Bill.

Bill doesn't call his girlfriend "bae."

He knows "bae" is Danish for "poop."

Bill is smart.
Be like Bill.

This is Bill.

Bill doesn't put his own made-up, stupid quotes under every photo he uploads on social networking sites.

He knows he is not yet a celebrity or famous enough to do that.

Bill is not a delusional fool.

Be like Bill.

This is Bill.

Bill likes to eat meat.

But he doesn't hate vegans and vegetarians because they don't.

He knows everyone can eat whatever they want.

Bill respects their choices.

Be like Bill.

This is Bill.

Bill goes to school.

Bill isn't rude to his teachers because he knows they are not paid much and are just there to help him learn.

Bill treats them with respect and is thankful for them.

Be like Bill.

This is Bill.

Bill is on Facebook.

He doesn't message every hot girl he sees on his news feed.

Bill knows it annoys the girls and makes him look like a creep.

Bill isn't desperate.

Be like Bill.

This is Bella.

Bella doesn't remove her eyebrows and draw them back on.

She knows that makes her look ridiculous.

Bella is smart.
Be like Bella.

This is Bill.

Bill proposed to a girl and she rejected his proposal.

Bill still respects her and she does not become a tramp all of a sudden.

Bill is above that.
Be like Bill.

This is Bill.

Bill travels a lot around the world.

Despite doing so, Bill doesn't check in on Facebook with every new location he visits.

Bill isn't smug.

Be like Bill.

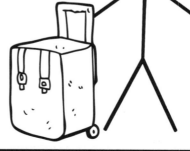

This is Bill.

Bill meets a new girl online and they like each other so they swap phone numbers.

He doesn't then immediately proceed to send her photos of his genitals.

Bill is not a pervert.

Be like Bill.

This is Bill.

Bill borrowed some money from a friend.

Bill paid him back and thanked him for it as soon as he could.

Bill values friendship more than money.

Bill is a good friend.
Be like Bill.

This is Bella.

Bella is on Facebook.

She likes to play games like Candy Crush.

Bella doesn't send all her friends game requests though.

She knows no one gives a damn.

Bella isn't annoying.

Be like Bella.

This is Bill

Bill sees something on the Internet that is offensive to him.

He doesn't react and simply moves on as he knows arguing on the internet is pointless.

Bill is smart.
Be like Bill.

This is Bill.

Bill doesn't hide his last seen on WhatsApp.

Bill wants people to know when he is avoiding them.

He has nothing to hide.

Bill is honest.
Be like Bill.

This is Bella.

Bella is in the bathroom.

Bella doesn't spend time taking 45 selfies.

She uses the bathroom for its purpose.

Bella is smart.
Be like Bella.

This is Bill.

Bill loves listening to music.

He buys the songs instead of searching for free downloads on the Internet.

Bill supports the music industry.

Be like Bill.

This is Bill.

Bill is on Instagram but he doesn't write "Follow for Follow" on his bio.

He knows that makes him look like a spammy moron.

Bill has a life.

Be like Bill.

This is Bill.

Bill likes to work out and goes to the gym regularly.

He has a well-toned body.

But he doesn't upload naked pictures of himself every day on social media sites and call others fat.

Bill isn't a douche.

Be like Bill.

This is Bill

Bill doesn't annoy his friends by asking stupid questions.

He simply Googles them instead.

Bill isn't a lazy wuss.

Be like Bill.

This is Bill.

Bill knows the difference between they're, there, and their.

Bill is intelligent.
Be like Bill.

This is Bill.

Bill just woke up.

Bill took a selfie.

Bill doesn't post it on Facebook writing, "I'm so ugly today," because if he really felt like that he wouldn't have posted it.

Bill doesn't need anyone to tell him he's handsome.

Be like Bill.

This is Bill.

Bill has a crush on a girl.

He just mans up and tells her instead of writing clues on Facebook.

Bill is a brave guy.
Be like Bill.

This is Bill.

Bill takes a selfie.

He uploads it to social networking sites.

But Bill doesn't use hashtags for #every #single #word #he #writes because he knows that's annoying as hell.

Bill isn't a jerk.

Be like Bill.

This is Bill.

Bill notices someone has made a grammatical mistake online.

He just moves on and doesn't insult them for making the mistake.

Bill isn't a grammar Nazi.

Be like Bill.

This is Bill.

When Bill goes shopping, he checks the expiration date of items before buying them.

Bill is alert.
Be like Bill.

This is Bill.

Bill is studying in the library at the university.

He talks quietly so he doesn't disturb the other students.

Bill is respectful.

Be like Bill.

This is Bill.

Bill sees a woman breast-feeding her baby in public.

He doesn't get disgusted or offended by this act.

Bill knows it's a natural part of life.

Bill is understanding.

Be like Bill.

This is Bill.

Bill eats "healthy" food and so do his kids.

He doesn't feel the need to brag about this on Facebook by posting pics of his dinner every day with obscure hashtags.

Bill knows no one gives a damn.

Bill is sensible.

Be like Bill.

This is Bill.

Bill sees Facebook telling him to change his profile picture.

He has got a mind of his own and doesn't bother.

Bill decides for himself.

Be like Bill.

This is Bill.

Bill enjoys playing FIFA with his friends.

But he doesn't watch replays of every bloody goal he scores against them.

Bill knows that annoys his friends.

Bill is smart.
Be like Bill.

This is Bill.

Bill is chatting with his girlfriend on WhatsApp.

She answers with "K."

Bill knows he's screwed.

Bill is realistic.
Be like Bill.

This is Bill.

Bill knows 1 + 1 equals 2 and not 11.

Bill is a genius.
You can never be like Bill.

About the Authors

Eugeniu Croitoru is a twenty-four-year-old currently based in Milan, Italy. He manages a lot of popular Facebook pages, including the Be Like Bill page (OfficialBLB). His dream is to become an Internet entrepreneur, and writing this book is the first major step toward making his dream come true.

Debabrata Nath is a twenty-six-year-old from Guwahati, India, who has been a geek all of his life. Computers and video games have always been his first love and all of his work revolves around them. Apart from managing the Be Like Bill Facebook page, he is also the cofounder of one of the biggest gaming media sites in the world, Fraghero (www.fraghero.com).